HOW TO DEAL WITH DIFFICULT PEOPLE

Learn How to Effectively Communicate and End Conflict With Difficult People

(The Ultimate Guide to Getting Along With Everyone)

Christine Hale

Published by Sharon Lohan

© **Christine Hale**

All Rights Reserved

How to Deal With Difficult People: Learn How to Effectively Communicate and End Conflict With Difficult People (The Ultimate Guide to Getting Along With Everyone)

ISBN 978-1-990334-73-3

All rights reserved. No part of this guide may be reproduced in any form without permission in writing from the publisher except in the case of brief quotations embodied in critical articles or reviews.

Legal & Disclaimer

The information contained in this book is not designed to replace or take the place of any form of medicine or professional medical advice. The information in this book has been provided for educational and entertainment purposes only.

The information contained in this book has been compiled from sources deemed reliable, and it is accurate to the best of the Author's knowledge; however, the Author cannot guarantee its accuracy and validity and cannot be held liable for any errors or omissions. Changes are periodically made to this book. You must consult your doctor or get professional medical advice before using any of the suggested remedies, techniques, or information in this book.

Upon using the information contained in this book, you agree to hold harmless the Author from and against any damages, costs, and expenses, including any legal fees potentially resulting from the application of any of the information provided by this guide. This disclaimer applies to any damages or injury caused by the use and application, whether directly or indirectly, of any advice or information presented, whether for breach of contract, tort, negligence, personal injury, criminal intent, or under any other cause of action.

You agree to accept all risks of using the information presented inside this book. You need to consult a professional medical practitioner in order to ensure you are both able and healthy enough to participate in this program.

Table of Contents

INTRODUCTION 1

CHAPTER 1: WORKING ON YOUR FOCUS 4

CHAPTER 2: HOW TO APPROACH DIFFICULT PEOPLE 9

CHAPTER 3: HOW TO REPRIMAND EFFECTIVELY 16

CHAPTER 4: HOW TO DEAL WITH DIFFICULT PEOPLE AT HOME 41

CHAPTER 5: KILL THE DIFFICULT PERSON WITH KINDNESS 45

CHAPTER 6: BUILDING A RESILIENT MINDSET 49

CHAPTER 7: EFFECTIVE PHRASES THAT CAN BE USED 56

CHAPTER 8: THE MARTYR EMPLOYEE OR 'VICTIM' 85

CHAPTER 9: THE GUILT TRIPPER 95

CHAPTER 10: THE PRACTICAL WAYS TO WIN DIFFICULT PEOPLE OVER OR TO APPLY IN DEALING WITH THEM. .. 110

CHAPTER 11: HOW TO DEAL WITH A DIFFICULT CUSTOMER AND PROVIDE GREAT CUSTOMER SERVICE 125

CONCLUSION 129

Introduction

This book contains proven steps and strategies on how to effectively relate with and communicate with problematic colleagues, bosses, and subordinates.

Have you ever been bullied at work? Do you find yourself a victim of nasty rumors? Is a co-worker's negative behavior getting on your nerves? The thing about difficult people in the workplace is that ignoring them is just not enough. Leaving these issues unresolved can not only damage your livelihood but also diminish the pride and joy that you experience from your career.

When the office is beginning to feel a lot like hell, then it's time to take action. But where should you begin? In these pages, you will learn both non-confrontational and confrontational approaches to deal with problematic coworkers, superiors, and employees. Confrontations don't necessarily have to end up in brawls and catfights and lawsuits. There is always a way to handle each issue in a tactful and legal manner. If you're not used to handling confrontations, then you'll benefit from the valuable tips contained in the following chapters.

Difficult people in the work setting come in different shapes and sizes. There are those who undermine your work efforts while there are those who siphon your soul with their perpetual pessimism. This book will teach you strategies on how to deal with the different types of difficult people in the workplace. Whether your nemesis is a gossip monger, or a bully, or some genius perfectionist know-it-all, find out how you can deal with them while preserving your reputation and your sanity. Lastly, learn how to turn these potential enemies into possible allies that can help you reach your ultimate work goals.

Thanks again for downloading this book, I hope you enjoy it!

Chapter 1: Working On Your Focus

Focus on the specific situation that is making you feel frustrated. Tell them directly how you feel about what they are doing without trying to blame them.

Your aim is to define your feelings, not to cause further heat.

The art of focus is very important in order to achieve specific tone and to focus on specific topic even when you feel frustrated.

Always make your goals specific to the point

If you want to accomplish something right away, do not mix things up. Focus on a specific goal at a specific time.

Concentrate on your emotions and turn them into goals, to be achieved, and to improve with constant effort.

Embrace the boredom

Sometimes focusing on yourself might be boring and unadventurous but once you are able to stay as long as it is required, you will begin to see the benefits in real life.

Your decision-making skills will be purged once you are able to accept that the most important moment of life might still be boring.

Delete people

You need to once in a while stay away from human beings. Even the people that love and care about you might be frustrating.

They can be a total distraction to the way you want your mind to work. You need to isolate yourself once in a while in order to seek the needed balance.

Get a good night sleep

The importance of a good night sleep in creating a good and balanced brainpower cannot be overemphasized.

The aim is to make sure that your brain is well rested in order to develop a power towards insightful problem-solving.

You won't have to worry about being overwhelmed or feeling dumb whenever you are faced with a frustrating situation.

Embrace observation

Even if you are the leader, you should not rush to always act upon the occurrence of things.

You don't need to act immediately when a person says something to you. You need to be distant and calculating.

You need to observe how things are coming through. You need to be a spectator for a while in order to see things differently, and to take some good final decisions.

Train your brain to focus

Train your mental muscle to focus on things that matter. Only focus on things that will bring about benefit.

Try as much as possible to eliminated things or people that will keep you distracted.

Involve in activities that will help train your brain, starting from physical exercises.

Leave your emotions where you found them

Do not bring your work emotions to the doorstep of your home. Always leave work at work, and come back as the happy you.

Only worry about work or what is happening in the office when you are in the office.

Always finish what you need to finish and never take your frustrations to places they don't need to be.

Chapter 2: How To Approach Difficult People

Now that you have seen the different types of difficult people and their characteristics, let us now look at how to approach these types of people. By approach, we mean how to respond to a difficult person, and how to act around them. Below are some highlighted points detailing how to go about this:

1. Pause for a minute

Difficult people are mostly very provocative when you are in a conversation with them. Therefore, you need to learn how to calm your nerves when this happens. How can you do this? You can do this through taking deep breaths and a moment to calm your emotions and collect your thoughts before you reply to a question they may have asked. Doing this will help you settle your nerves and senses before you offer a reply quickly and say something you might later regret.

This technique can also slow down the rhythm of an argument. For example, when an aggressive person attacks you, he or she normally tries to provoke you into attacking them back. Immediately you do, they escalade the argument until you start acting like them. However, when you take frequent pauses to think, you diffuse their interest in arguing and abusing you since the abuse is not getting to you.

2. Keep your cool

Another effective way to approach a difficult person is by maintaining your cool. As we saw in the previous chapter, difficult people can come on strongly. They can call you names (stupid, idiot), make you look stupid, and even abuse you. This may sometimes be hard to swallow. To avoid sinking to their level, you must fight your anger and maintain your cool.

When you do this, the other person will eventually notice how ridiculous he or she sounds when yelling and reflect upon his or her actions. That way, you completely diffuse their intentions. You should definitely try this out the next time a difficult person comes on to you.

3. Choose your battles wisely

Whenever you find yourself in a situation where you might enter an argument with a difficult person, you should ask yourself if whatever you are talking about is worth fighting for. It may surprise you to discover you normally argue about nothing.

You should avoid arguing about things that do not add value to your life. Only engage in debates about things that are important to you and your life. For instance, you can have a constructive argument with your boss about how many hours you have worked. However, when it comes to arguing about who has a better phone; you can let that battle go.

4. Stick to the facts

Difficult people such as the complainer type easily trigger arguments. Therefore, you should be very careful not to say something wrong when you are talking with a difficult person. If you know that person's trigger topics, avoid talking these topics. A good example of this is if politics is a trigger for a friend. In this instance, when you are around that person, you can avoid this topic and stick to other topics.

Sometimes, you might encounter a difficult person who always finds something to argue about. In this scenario, limit your chat to facts. It might be difficult to make that person see your point of view, but you should not try to explain yourself in a bid to convince that person.

This process has been known to work and is highly effective when you are dealing with a difficult know it all person.

5. Assertively speak out for your rights and needs

Difficult people such as the know-it-all type usually want everything to go their way and do not believe you can teach them anything. When engaging with this type of person, talk more assertively. Talk with confidence and clarity.

When dealing with a partially know it all type of person, counter their uninformed thoughts by staying and playing it cool then correct their information. A good example is using words like. "I understand your frustrations on the slowness of this project. If I were you, I would be too. Unfortunately, this project normally takes time to complete."

6. Reduce interactions

Difficult people are everywhere and you will eventually have to deal with one at one time or the other. This may not be easy, but you can ease the pain of these encounters by, as much as is possible, avoiding, or reducing person-to-person interactions. When you have to interact with a difficult person, be as polite and positive as possible.

You can do this by keeping your conversations short whenever you bump into this type of person. Incase this fails, you can use other methods like excusing yourself after two minutes of conversation or inviting a third party who will make your conversation more bearable.

Tips on Dealing with Difficult People

The following are a couple of personal tips you can use when you frequently communicate with difficult people.

*Look for other positive relationships. This will balance your life by offsetting the negativity you receive from difficult people.

*When you are dealing with a difficult person, you will always encounter difficult moments. The best way to diffuse these moments is to add humor to them.

*You should be careful not to blame yourself or the other person because the difference in opinions and communication is a result of your personalities being different. Blame games will just make you bitter.

*Keep in mind that not everyone you talk to should be close to you. To get along with others, especially difficult people, you only need to be polite.

Chapter 3: How To Reprimand Effectively

It's fair to say that most managers don't like reprimanding employees; it's certainly not the most enjoyable part of the job. Indeed I'll go so far as to say those few bosses who do enjoy it are probably not very effective – or well liked!

Confrontation can be daunting for novice managers and those with experience alike, and yet it's a vital part of the job. The art of a good reprimand is to be constructive; you don't want the employee to end up demotivated and demoralised or their work will never improve.

According to workplace communications consultancy CHA, four out of 10 employees in the UK believe their organizations don't know how to constructively criticize. A similar number of those polled believe they don't know how to praise well either. We're not doing particularly well on either score, then.

So how should you rebuke or reprimand staff?

Personally, I like to use what we call "progressive discipline". I work from the basis that nearly all problem behavior can be corrected if it's caught early enough and handled effectively. It's a good mindset to get into; always focus on discipline as a way to improve employee performance and not to punish. Don't fall into the trap of thinking discipline is always done "to" an employee. It's much more effective to do it "with" an employee.

Your company may well have a formal discipline procedure in place, so you'll want to check with them first. Assuming they don't, you could try progressive discipline.

First up, if you have an employee who just isn't meeting the standards expected, take the time to counsel him or her, making sure they understand what is expected of them. You'll also want to determine if there are any issues that you are unaware of that are contributing to the problem and help to solve them.

If you still have the issue after that, your next step is to verbally reprimand the employee for their poor performance. We'll come onto how to do that in a minute. Following the verbal warning comes a written one, if needed a few days or weeks later, which will sit in their file.

After that, you need to consider your next step carefully; some managers like to suspend problem employees for a few days, others prefer to take the problem further up the line. If all else fails, however, you're going to have to think about termination.

I said that nearly all behaviour can be improved; I firmly believe that. The sad truth, however, is that a small proportion of the problem employees you deal with will never get better. You will have no choice but to terminate their employment.

Now HR rules actually make this pretty tough to do in the UK; managers often complain that they have to jump through so many hoops, they should join the circus. You'll want to take legal advice before you do anything, of course, but the good news is that progressive discipline pretty much does the job for you, or certainly helps you on your way, if it comes to that. It gives you a record of all discussion between you and the employee and substantial documentation to prove you have exhausted all other options – very valuable in this day and age where HR insists you must write down everything in duplicate, triplicate or, better yet, in blood!

On a personal note, while it is never a nice thing to have to terminate someone's employment, you do at least have the satisfaction of knowing you gave them more than one chance to improve. They just didn't take it.

So, if you do need to reprimand someone, how should you do it?

How to Reprimand

Don't let the small things go: It's occasionally tempting to let minor indiscretions go and not create a fuss, assuming they won't happen again. You may even think your team will thank you for it, recognizing that you are a benevolent boss. Unfortunately that's often not the case, I'm afraid. It's human nature to push the envelope a little; if you fail to check up on the small things, your team will assume you don't care or aren't on top of things and the bigger issues will start to slip as well. In contrast, the team will assume that a boss who checks up on the little things will check up on the big things too and will act accordingly.

Address problems as soon as possible. Don't let them fester. Too many of us want to put off potentially unpleasant tasks but that's not helping the employee or the team. If you don't immediately let the problem employee know their behaviour is out of line, or their results are under par, they'll assume that it's either okay or you don't care. Remember progressive discipline at all times. If you allow disciplinary action to wait, you'll need to start off by applying harsh sanctions when you do finally tackle it, as the problems have grown. That leaves you very little place to go before termination. Likewise, what seems like unfair or harsh disciplinary measures with no prior warning can destabilise the entire workforce and demoralise the team.

Do it in private. Never reprimand employees in front of their workmates. It's unprofessional. Don't do it by email either. Call them into your office or take them to one side to talk it over. Reprimanding someone in public not only embarrasses or humiliates the employee in front of their workmates, but it also demotivates other staff members around them who witness the telling off. It can lead to a climate of fear, where staff are afraid to take chances or use initiative because they are worried they will be next in line for a public reprimand. If you find yourself losing control of your temper and shouting at an employee in public, take a deep breath, calm yourself down and don't do it again. Walk away if necessary and then ask to speak to the employee in question later when you are calm and in control and do so in your office or away from other employees.

Make enough time: Make sure you give the situation enough time. You may be tempted to get it over with as quickly as possible, but that's not really being fair to the employee.

Don't beat around the bush. There's a common line of thought that calls for managers to "sandwich" the bad news in with the good. The management gurus encourage you to find something positive to say as you open the meeting – "I thought your work on x went well" – before getting to the problem discussion, "However your work on y had a few problems" before making sure you eventually end on a positive note again, "I'm sure your work on z will be great".

I have to be honest; for many scenarios, I HATE, hate, hate the sandwich technique. It just doesn't work. It sends conflicting messages and often the employee isn't exactly sure what point you're trying to make. If the news is uniformly bad, don't use the sandwich technique. You want them to know that there's a problem here. Be upfront with them; don't short change them. You'll keep their respect if you're honest. What's more, you're giving them a genuine chance to change; the danger with the "sandwich" technique is that they won't know how much of a problem they have until you suddenly take more draconian measures. That's demoralising and letting the employee down, quite frankly.

One quick point to make here however: let me just stress that reprimanding someone shouldn't be the only time you talk to them. You don't want the employee to feel that no-one ever says anything good to them; if you hear this complaint during a reprimand, you're neglecting another crucial element of your job - giving praise where it is due. A good manager reprimands when needed, but also goes out of their way to praise and give positive feedback when employees deserve it. Any employee who only hears bad news is being let down by their manager. Don't be afraid to praise an employee; it's especially important to do so if they have previously been reprimanded and you can see a subsequent improvement in their work; you want to give positive reinforcement.

Another quick point - don't forget that you are not reprimanding someone to punish them; you are doing so to help improve their work. As such, reprimands can be a positive thing, which brings me onto my next point...

Focus on the work and not the person. Be specific, give concrete examples of what the person did and didn't do. Focus on one or two key areas only; don't reel off a list. Likewise, don't make it a personal attack. Show respect at all times.

Avoid "I" and "You". Like I said, discipline is not something done to the employee; it should be done with them. Use "we" instead.

Be positive: Suggest ways that the employee can improve in the future; remember not to put his or her work down, but find ways to be constructive about the areas you need them to improve upon.

Allow time for the message to sink in and then allow them to respond. You'll have to judge their explanations or excuses by the employee themselves. If they have a spotless record until now, you might want to give them the benefit of the doubt. If they're known for making excuses however, you might want to take the latest one with a pinch of salt and keep a close eye on him or her.

Look for root causes: As I said earlier, try to ascertain if there is any root cause to the problem; do they lack the skills necessary, do they have underlying personal or psychological problems? If you can identify these, you can tackle them. If you miss the root cause, however, the problem is unlikely to get better unless the employee can address it by themselves.

Seek agreement of corrective action for the future. The whole point of disciplinary action is to gain agreement to change; you want a positive outcome and a pledge that things will be different. So what should you do if the employee in question refuses to make eye contact, fiddles with their clothing and generally gives you the silent treatment while you are trying to discipline them? The first thing to be aware of is that everyone handles criticism differently; some will become defensive, others belligerent, others still will deny everything while some employees do the opposite and admit their failings. Some people might even cry, while others, like our example here, become morose and disconnected. The fact is that you are not going to know whether they are deliberately giving you the silent treatment in protest or if they are too embarrassed to look you in the eye. As such, give them the benefit of the doubt. Point out that you want a two-way conversation and they will need to participate; ask them outright for their views and ask them if they agree with your points. Stress that the issues have to be addressed together or you will be forced to take further action. Give them all the opportunity to respond. If they still don't talk, only you can judge whether they are being deliberately surly or if they may need more time to process. It could, of course, be that they don't want to talk there and then because they are worried they will be emotional. If so, give them more time. Rearrange the meeting for the next day when they have had time to deal with their initial shock but stress that you would like a plan of action from them when you do meet again.

Monitor and give feedback: If the employee agrees to make specific improvements, make sure you monitor it and give feedback. If they refuse or reject your criticisms, whether in your initial meeting or the next one (or they continue to give you the silent treatment as in the above example) you'll need to take it to the next level. This is where your progressive discipline comes in again. If an employee refuses to agree on the next steps to improvement - note, that doesn't necessarily mean they have to agree with all your points but they should at least pledge to try to tackle the problem - you can't let it slide. For the sake of discipline in your workplace, you need to tackle it. You need to go back to our sliding scale of progressive discipline and step up to the next level. You may need to give them a more formal warning, a suspension or finally even terminate them. An employee who refuses to agree to corrective action is also refusing to get any better or improve their work. Maybe then, they shouldn't be in your company. Follow the steps to progressive discipline and any company policies you have in place, give them plenty of notice and time to improve, but be prepared to let them go if you need to.

Be aware of your options before the disciplinary meeting; if they refuse there and then to agree a corrective course of action, let them know that you are not happy with the outcome of your meeting and will come back to them about the next steps you wish to take. Give both of you some time to calm down and think. Then call them in the next day and issue your formal warning or whatever course of action you deem appropriate. Hopefully, once they realise how seriously you are taking the problem, they may think again and agree to step up.

If you can, try to end with a positive note. This is not the "sandwich" technique; it could be something as simple as reiterating the corrective action you have hopefully just put in place and the next steps the employee will take. This shows that you are looking forwards and not backwards and are prepared to give them another chance to improve. This is a positive attitude. Of course, in some cases such as our example above where an employee refuses to agree corrective action, it's almost impossible to end on a positive note and that's ok. You don't want to end on a positive note if you still have real issues to deal with; further disciplinary action is due and you want the employee to know how seriously you take that.

Don't hold the reprimand over them: Once you have completed the reprimand, don't change your behaviour towards the employee or treat them any differently the next day. Treat them as you did before, with the caveat that you must obviously monitor their behaviour and give feedback. Show them that you are willing to give them the chance to improve and don't hold a grudge against them. Demonstrate this overtly; otherwise your employee may now feel awkward in your presence and imagine that they will never be able to get past this. You need to show them that as long as their work improves in the way that you agreed, there doesn't need to be a problem. Lead by example and be professional; this ideally shows the employee that there is nothing to dwell on or to sulk about. If you do have an employee who sulks after your disciplinary meeting, take the high road. Treat them as you would any other employee; ignore their sulking and act professional as always. It may be tempting to tell them to stop sulking but you need to be careful not to look as if you are now picking on that member of staff for the sake of it; should they later lodge a complaint about you, it's hard to prove specifics on something as vague as sulking. Hopefully the sulking will cease in a short while. If it doesn't, however, then you may need to speak to the employee about their attitude. Combine it with a feedback meeting and make it another target that they have to address. The good thing about sulking is that it doesn't usually last forever.

When you speak to problem employees, keep in mind a couple of key things:

First, I'm going to repeat myself here because it's important: make sure that you don't only speak to your team or employees when there's a problem. Remember what our poll said above – we don't praise enough either. So, make the effort to praise them when they do well. Remember the phrase "criticise in private, praise in public."

Secondly, never reprimand an employee when you are angry; wait until you have calmed down. This is another reason why you should never ignore problem behaviour; chances are that if you allow it to continue unchecked over a long period of time, you will have built up an animosity to the employee concerned. In short, you are likely to be angry with them. That reprimand discussion is therefore not going to go well.

You may also have some employees who get insulted or offended far too easily and see slights where there really aren't any. The only thing you can do with these employees is to reiterate that you are talking about their work and not anything personal and to be professional with them; stay calm and make it clear that you expect a professional response back from them too.

Should you shout at an employee?

We all know employers who shout to be heard; who scream, swear and yell at employees for every little mistake. It may even seem as if they get things done; after all, some employees seem to work better when they're scared of the boss. But is that the sort of boss you really want to be? Do you want people to respect you or fear you? It's very rare that you can have both.

Bosses who shout at their team are often universally loathed; morale is low and far from motivating employees, a boss who shouts at them often demotivates other people to only do the basic amount of work needed to get by and 'avoid detection'. Screaming at someone rarely motivates them in the long term. If you shout at your employees, you are creating a toxic work environment and I guarantee you that you'll end up with a high employee turnover. It may make an employee 'jump to it' there and then, but they - and everyone else around them -

will start looking for new jobs pretty soon if that sort of treatment continues.

A boss who needs to shout to get employees to do something isn't actually a very good manager. I'd go as far as to say that they're a pretty weak manager actually. You tend to find that bosses who need to shout lack man-management skills - in short, they're not good with people. You can have strong discipline without resorting to bullying tactics which, after all, is what shouting is.

At the very least, a manager who shouts and screams at the team doesn't have a very good hold on his or her temper. Could that be you? In the fast-paced high-pressured you're-only-as-good-as-your-last-job environment of today, staying calm isn't always easy. There often seems to be so much relying on each and every task that even the slightest thing could threaten a catastrophe. As the one responsible for holding it all together, it's not surprising that you may sometimes struggle to control your emotions. If this sounds familiar, let me tell you one thing right now: you're not helping anyone, least of all yourself, by screaming at your employees. If you find yourself wanting to shout at them, you have to realise that you're probably stressed. I could write a whole other book about how to deal with stress! Needless to say, you need to find an outlet outside of work to relax and chill; take a good long look at your work-life balance and make changes if work threatens to take over your life. Try to remind yourself that work, while important, is not the be all and end all. If you do find yourself struggling to control a temper, recognise when to walk away. Go back to your office and close the door or find somewhere to have some private time; perhaps get out of the work environment and go for a walk around the block. Calm down, count to 10 and breathe deeply, whatever works. If you find yourself regularly getting anxious, stressed or angry, avoid alcohol and caffeine and admit that you have a problem. Consider if you need anger management lessons; some anger is normal but constant anger is not. Always conduct disciplinary conversations when you are calm.

Reprimands should ideally be used to 'steer' the ship and give it a nudge in the right direction every now and then, as opposed to being a day-to-day default attitude. If you tackle problems before they become larger issues, you should never need to 'scare' an employee into submission. Likewise, if you also work hard at staff motivation, as all good managers should, you should ideally know what motivates individual team members and can appeal to them on that level before they ever become problem employees. If an employee still doesn't react well to orders without shouting, however, you need to take them through the progressive disciplinary procedure to show them you mean business. Doing this, as opposed to shouting, shows you are professional and that the disciplinary procedure isn't personal.

Don't assume that you can shout at just one problem employee either, even if you think he or she will react better if they're scared. Shouting at them to get a task done doesn't solve the underlying problem with that worker, does it? The only way you can continue to make sure that they perform adequately is to continue shouting at them... and that affects everyone around them as well. Other people will witness the intimidation, may assume you are picking on the employee in question even if you think it is warranted, the atmosphere will turn and before you know it, you'll have a toxic working environment. That's when everyone becomes desperate to leave.

Oh and one other thing - bullying bosses invariably get reported to HR in the end!

Discipline doesn't have to be a big confrontation; it can be as simple as a few words if you address it early and communicate frequently. You've got to be cruel to be kind; it's an old cliché but an apt one for this situation.

A sign of a good manager is someone who hardly ever has to reprimand their staff because every single member of the team already knows what is expected of them and delivers. That's the sort of work environment you want.

Chapter 4: How To Deal With Difficult People At Home

The people who live with you at home would either be family or flat mates. These are permanent characters in your life and will not be easily changed. Because they surround your personal life on an everyday basis, they affect your lives in enduring ways.

You would know their personalities in more depth and more likely than not, you're already accustomed to them that you're more skillful in dealing with these people already. However, because they are consistent players in your everyday routine, they may be more difficult to deal with. Simple quirks that are unnoticed in other people will annoy you severely because you are exposed to these habits every single day.

Similarly, dealing with them will be quite different.

Stay out of the way

It would be best to stay clear in critical conditions. You would be familiar when these personalities are heightened and when you are more susceptible to react negatively to these. It could be when you've had an especially tough day at work, during certain times of the week or month, or when sick.

Since you are able to see the warning signs, it would be the smartest thing to do to avoid conflict entirely.

Don't aggravate things

When you fail on the attempt to dodge the clash, do your best to stretch your calm and try not to react on impulse. However you handle the situation, keep in mind that your primary goal should be keeping yourself from adding fuel to the fire.

Don't be pushy

People have different ideas of right and wrong. Just because our personalities differ from each other doesn't make us right and them wrong, or vice versa. What keeps our relationships strong is mutual respect that there we are all different in some ways.

While we try out best to nudge each other towards personal growth, development, all for the better, it would not do well to be pushy and force upon others our own ideas. When done carelessly, this might trigger a bigger fight.

Don't alienate them

Too much of anything is bad. On the other end of the spectrum, don't become too indifferent either. This might seem like you're alienating them already and think that you don't value them in your life.

Moderation is key. Showing that you care is a valuable part of any relationship.

Because of the role that they play in your life, you must be more delicate in handling difficult people at home. It would make your life very complicated to disrupt these relationships because they are such integral parts of who you are as a person.

As important as these they are, relationships with family and close friends also have a natural way of healing themselves. It is with the having fights you've had growing up and mending them overtime that no grudges are held and that forgiveness is easily given.

Chapter 5: Kill The Difficult Person With Kindness

Now, if you have not succeeded in opening that door with words of kindness or commonalities, then it is time to bring in the big guns. Have you ever heard the term "Random Acts of Kindness?" These are acts that people perform for other people without any particular reason other than just being kind. It is also important to know that this is also done without any thought of "What's in it for me?"

It is along the line of "paying it forward," like the movie, where the teacher taught the kids the lesson of when someone does something kind for you, you should in turn do something nice for somebody else. This method should work for any of the difficult people you might have to deal with in your life.

If this person is in your family, it is easy to do a kindness for someone you love. Just doing little things with a reminder that I did this "Just because I love you." A hot meal, a magazine or book, a dessert, an ice cream cone—who does not love ice cream?! Or just spend a little time with a family member who needs a friend. Offer to baby sit or adult-sit, give someone who is overstressed a little break. There are so many ways to help someone with a sad heart. And do you know who else will feel better? I am sure you know who I mean!

If the difficult one is your neighbor, a random act of kindness is taking over a plate of cookies or brownies, shovel their walk when it snows, if you have a teenager, give him or her a few dollars to help the neighbor with their lawn or garbage cans. None of that is too much to offer someone. Consider that some day, you might be old or disabled and how much a random act like that would mean to you.

At work, if the words of kindness didn't strike a chord, then do nice things for that person. Regardless if it is your boss or a coworker whom you must work with every day, they are not immune to those random acts of kindness. Bring in the donuts; offer to stay late if your department is overwhelmed. Offer to take on extra work; offer to do anything you can do to help. Be the sunshine committee—make birthday cards, holiday cards, organize get-togethers that will encourage employees to show respect and learn how to communicate with each other.

If doing these things will make your life a little more bearable, isn't that worth the little bit of effort it takes to make your job a better place to work? Make your house a happier place to live. And most of all, make the world a better place for us all! If you set the example of kindness, it soon catches on. And before too long, life seems better. Things come back to you twofold when you do kind things for others.

Think of being on the other side of the act. How can you think of being mean or snappy to someone who is showing a kindness to you? One would have to be a real ogre to be like that. But, there are always the Scrooges of the modern world, aren't there? So, what do we do with people like that? Easy question, difficult answer...

Chapter 6: Building A Resilient Mindset

To effectively deal with difficult personalities, you have to develop a resilient mindset. Resilience is the ability to cope with daily life stresses without losing your cool. Resilient individuals are rarely troubled by other people's behavior and as such, they tend to excel. They overcome any challenge they face due to other people being difficult.

Change your script

We sometimes respond the same way to situations we perceive to be difficult even without taking the specific circumstances into consideration. We blindly follow the same script every time. For instance, some people will react to a person who is yelling by yelling back. This is ingrained in them and they know no other way of dealing with this situation. We should change our behavior in the face of difficulty. Our attitude might be fueling a situation from bad to worse. Aim first to understand where this person is coming from and what their real intentions are. Do they want to get a specific reaction from us? Might they be interested in obstructing us and bringing us down? Are they going through a hard time in their life? When we understand a person, we put ourselves in the best position to respond to them in a way that will be beneficial mostly to us but even to them.

Be stress hardy

Stress hardy people have developed a sense of what's important in life and what's not. They spend their time and energy on only what will improve their lives. All other side shows are shoved aside. They have no skills to deal with a negative or difficult person. They understand that difficult situations and difficult people are a part of life and you'll encounter them along the way but they don't dwell on them. They confront them as soon as they can to minimize the impact of such kind of people on their daily activities. When you don't have control over a situation, you let it pass but when you can influence the outcome of another situation, no matter how difficult people you are dealing with may prove to be.

View a situation from the perspective of others

To be resilient, you have to be ready to view issues from a different perspective. You need to be empathizing to other people and try to understand where they are coming from. Most people don't just decide to be difficult, they might not even think of themselves as such. Their mode of understanding of an issue might be different from yours. For instance, people from different cultures might have a completely different perspective on an issue. Understanding means putting yourself in the other person shoes. You should always behave the same way you expect people to behave towards you.

Communication

A single word at the right time can avert a disaster that was about to happen. In dealing with difficult people, you should always strive to communicate effectively. Communication comes in two ways, verbal and nonverbal. Verbal is the most obvious but a lot of communication happens through nonverbal means as well. You need to learn how to decode nonverbal communication. Some people will not say a word to you but they'll still trouble you. This is common in the workplace where a colleague will just be uncooperative and fail to communicate even when you are supposed to be working together. You also need to learn how to pass on information through nonverbal means. Some nonverbal cues include posture, eye movement, facial expressions and use of hands. Listen actively to both the verbal and nonverbal means to get the full reaction. Some common barriers to effective communication are assumption that the message is received and understood, use of a wrong medium, lack of emotions when delivering the message, communication by intimidation, and use of the wrong communication style

Accept others the way they are

If you are to be resilient, you have to understand others and accept them the way they are without expecting them to change. By accepting others, you understand their strengths and weaknesses and how best to respond to them. Accepting someone involves having realistic expectation of their behavior. If you have prior information that you are dealing with a difficult person, you should expect it and be prepared for it.

Adapting to change

Being able to adapt to change is one of the character traits of resilient people. In all spheres of life, change is now occurring at very fast rate and any person especially leaders who are unable or unwilling to adapt to it, find themselves having trouble dealing with different kinds of people. This change brings about new opportunities, more effective ways of carrying out tasks and greater efficiency at the workplace.

Low levels of anxiety

To be resilient in life and in the workplace, you have low levels of anxiety. The human nature wants us to remain where we are used to. We are most comfortable doing things we have been doing as this brings about a sense of security. However, if we remain doing these things, we might be left behind in our fast paced world. Anxiety is the number one reason that holds people back from implementing something new. Anxiety is mostly driven by negative emotions, past unpleasant experiences, or even fear of the unknown.

Chapter 7: Effective Phrases That Can Be Used

Have you dealt with someone who seems so unreasonable that you ask, "Hey, what's up with that guy?" In this chapter we're going to take a look at how people like Mr. Potter and Patti's mom are wired and what makes them tick. Then we'll examine how to accurately assess the unreasonable person so we can deal with him or her effectively. Conflict with unreasonable people goes well only when we first know and understand what we're up against.

Unreasonable People Are Everywhere

Unreasonable people are called many things. Several of the terms contain swear words, refer to body parts, or deliberately insult the person's ancestry. We've all heard them, and most of us have used them on occasion. The list that follows is by no means exhaustive but includes some of the common terms, omitting the more tasteless ones.

big baby	loon	prima donna
bull in a china shop	loony bird	psycho
bully	loser	schmuck
control freak	martyr	smooth operator
crazy-maker	messiah	snake in the grass
creep	moron	turkey
drama queen	nut	victim
freak show	nut case	wacko
guilt tripper	pain in the neck	weasel
horse's tail	personality disorder	wolf in sheep's

jerk   piece of work   clothing

If unreasonable people are despotic rulers of nations, we call them "mad men." In the Bible, they are called "fools" or "the wicked." Unfortunately, we encounter unreasonable people throughout life. They first show up as toddlers throwing temper tantrums. At that point, the unreasonable person is a kid who needs to mature—to develop better ways of handling frustration. The ones who don't mature (for various reasons) show up again in elementary school as bullies on the playground. Again, the need is to grow—to learn more mature ways of dealing with peers. Those who fail to mature become adults who are called the names just mentioned. The unreasonable person is a child in an adult's body, a person who needs to grow up—to learn more mature ways of handling relationships and conflict.

Unreasonable people truly are everywhere, and a large percentage of the population meets the criteria we'll be discussing. We run into them at work, at school, at church, in the community, at the doctor's office, in government, in entertainment, at family gatherings, and in marriages. In fact, there are sleeper cells of unreasonable people all over the place. The following descriptive phrases are commonly used in reference to unreasonable people:

arrogant	going mental	repugnant
audacious	high maintenance	self-important
complex	high schoolish	sick
confusing	insecure	slimy
crazy	insufferable	stubborn
crazy as a loon	irritating	toxic

difficult	loony	treacherous
disordered	manipulative	two-faced
ego-centric	narcissistic	wacked
full of it	psychotic	

Joyce Landorf Heatherly referred to unreasonable people as "irregular."1 Susan Forward refers to them as "emotional blackmailers."2 Henry Cloud and John Townsend call them "unsafe."3 Scott Peck refers to them as "evil."4 Sometimes the word "political" is used, usually in a pejorative sense, communicating the idea that the people are two-faced, back-biting, power-hungry, self-advancing, conniving, and duplicitous. Hence, someone will say, "I didn't want to be on that board because it's so political." Jimmy Stewart, who played the title character in another Frank Capra film, Mr. Smith Goes to Washington, encountered the worst form of politics when he arrived in the nation's capital. Patriotism had attracted him to the nobility of public service, but he was depressingly disillusioned after discovering that some of his most idealized heroes were drastically different people in private than what they appeared to be in public—one of the chief characteristics of unreasonable people.

We are simultaneously fascinated by and frustrated with unreasonable people. We make movies about them, write books about them, and keep up with them through the tabloids. They are often people with dazzling positives alongside glaring negatives, and it's that mix of opposing traits that makes them so interesting and confounding. We often make one or more of the following statements about an unreasonable person:

He has some screws loose.

She thinks the world revolves around her.

She'll stab you in the back.

He creeps me out.

She wears me out.

There's one in every crowd.

She's never wrong about anything.

When she fights, she shows her true colors.

He gives me the heebie jeebies.

Here comes Joe, hide!

Once you're on her bad side, you can't get back.

He's always got an angle.

She thinks everyone's out to get her.

She sucks all the air out of the room.

He thinks the rules don't apply to him.

Being around her is a real soap opera.

Joe's wife has got to be a saint.

Unreasonable People Haven't Grown Up

The house I grew up in was next to a neighborhood park, and one of my playmates, Hector, lived across the field. He and I would play in the park with other kids from the neighborhood. Several things stand out in my memories about Hector. First, I had never known anyone else with that name. Second, he always wore the same pair of dirty, untied tennis shoes. Third, he drooled a lot and wiped it with a handkerchief his mom had given him. Finally, he was always smiling, and we had lots of fun.

This story probably makes you feel good if it conjures up pleasant memories from your own childhood. But I left out an important piece of information. Hector was in his twenties back then. He had a condition that left him mentally and physically impaired. His shoes were untied because he couldn't tie them. He drooled because he was unable to control his saliva. He was happy playing with little children because his own mental development had stalled at the level of a small child.

Now how do you feel about the story? Hector, it turns out, was chronologically old but developmentally young. It's tragic when a discrepancy exists between the two.

Unreasonable people have that sort of discrepancy. While it's true that everyone has maturity gaps, unreasonable people have pervasive impairments in their abilities to handle people problems. Some of the parts that are needed to flex and adjust in conflict situations didn't develop along with the rest of the parts, leaving them inflexible and rigid, lacking the "give and take" possessed by reasonable people. They are grown-ups who haven't grown up.

Why They Stopped Growing

Frequently a reasonable person being driven crazy by an unreasonable person will ask me, "What do you think is wrong with him?" That's hard to say. The problem could have an internal cause, such as something genetic or a brain malfunction that developed later in life (nature). Or it could have to do with external factors, such as having a deficient upbringing (nurture). Or it could be the result of his choices (what he's done with nature and nurture). Often it's a combination of factors. For whatever reason, the unreasonable person passed up or missed opportunities to grow up, becoming chronologically older while remaining developmentally young. He or she is now a child in a grown-up's body.

What Stopped Growing

Reasonable people have these muscles, which become stronger with use. If two reasonable people argue and handle their flaws well, they are likely to reach a resolution. Unreasonable people don't have some or all of these muscles. They never developed them, or they've become atrophied from years of disuse.

Unreasonable people have an aversion to personal wrongness that extends far beyond anything experienced by reasonable people. To them, being wrong presents a threat to survival that equals most physical threats. Unreasonable people put all of their energy into safeguarding rightness—to staying safe—and none into solving conflict problems. They're not interested in solving problems if doing so requires the acknowledgment of wrongness.

Let's look at the five "reason muscles" and what they look like in unreasonable people. Remember, having these muscles and using them is what distinguishes a reasonable person from someone who is not.

The Humility Muscle

The first muscle needed to handle wrongness well is the humility muscle, which gives a person the ability to acknowledge potential personal wrongness. When reasonable people use this muscle, the stance is, "I could be wrong, you could be right, let's talk." Reasonable people, who have healthy humility muscles, can handle being wrong if being right requires sacrificing the truth. They believe, though perhaps reluctantly, in the maxim, "Truth is your best ally." It may be painful to acknowledge wrongness, but they'll do so because being truthful has a higher value to them than being right.

Unwilling to allow for the possibility of wrongness, unreasonable people will sacrifice truth if being truthful means being wrong. They'll even lie to avoid being wrong. In fact, some unreasonable people revise truth so routinely that they delude themselves and come to believe their own revisions. The stance taken is, "I'm right, you're wrong, end of discussion." They can be arrogant and inflexible. That's why you can't reason with them. Your attempts at reasonableness won't work because they're not interested in reason; they're only interested in winning or in being right.

The Awareness Muscle

The second muscle needed is the awareness muscle, which enables us to observe areas of actual personal wrongness. Having this muscle, the reasonable person's stance is, "I see where I'm wrong." They see their strengths but also understand their weaknesses. Unreasonable people have ruled out the possibility of wrongness, so the stance taken is, "I only see where I'm right." Unreasonable people are notoriously lacking in self-awareness, not seeing the flaws in themselves that others so clearly see. Therefore, when problems occur, they automatically assume that others caused them.

The press box is the part of our personalities that enables us to make big-picture self-observations. For unreasonable people, the wires connecting the press box to the sidelines phones are severed. They don't have press box conversations and are sorely lacking in awareness. That's why we say:

She has no idea how she comes across.

He's a bull in a china shop.

He's clueless about the part he played in that argument.

Her husband sees it, her kids see it, her boss sees it. Everybody sees it but her.

She's oblivious.

Relationships are like mirrors in which we catch glimpses of the good and bad parts of ourselves. Reasonable people make use of the feedback that relationships provide. But unreasonable people catch no reflections of their flaws in relational mirrors.

The Responsibility Muscle

Sometimes referred to as a conscience, the responsibility muscle enables us to be bothered by personal wrongness. Unreasonable people are weak in the conscience department. While the reasonable person observes personal faults and cringes, the unreasonable person shrugs when flaws are pointed out. His or her stance is, "If I'm wrong, so what?"

One Sunday afternoon I sat riveted to a documentary about a well-known American who was great in public but not so great in private. With the passage of time, his once-concealed infidelities have become part of the historical record. A family friend was interviewed who recounted a conversation in which she asked him why he would take such chances and jeopardize his legacy. In response he calmly replied, "I guess I just can't help it." She then made this astute observation:

He always lived his life in compartments. There was the public compartment, in which he accomplished these great things, all of which were true. But he also had an unseen compartment in which he was repeatedly unfaithful to his wife and children. I think he knew there were discrepancies between the compartments, but they just didn't bother him that much.

In effect, the unreasonable person looks in the mirror, sees the glob of spinach on his teeth, doesn't like what he sees, and decides to quit looking in mirrors. The reasonable person seeks out truth to change for the better. The unreasonable person runs from truth to avoid discomfort.

The Empathy Muscle

The fourth muscle needed is the empathy muscle. Empathy is the ability to be bothered if our personal wrongness hurts others. It enables us to understand the effects we have on the other person and to use that understanding to govern our words and actions.

When a reasonable person uses this muscle, the resulting stance is, "It bothers me when my wrongness hurts you." He allows that understanding to shape how he behaves toward others. The unreasonable person is empathy deficient.

His stance is, "I'm only bothered when your wrongness hurts me." Consequently, the unreasonable person is often described as "cruel" or "insensitive" in his dealings with others. That's why we say, "It's all about him" or "I can't believe she could say (or do) that" or "Watch out, he'll stab you in the back." The unreasonable person gives little consideration to the impact of his words and actions on others. Reciprocal empathy is a realistic expectation in conflict with reasonable people. With unreasonable people, however, we should anticipate self-serving motivation and behaviors.

The Reliability Muscle

The reliability muscle is the ability to correct personal wrongness. A reasonable person is bothered by his flaws and determines, "When I'm wrong, I'll change." Since the unreasonable person fails to see his flaws, he is neither bothered by them nor sees the need to correct them. Consequently, his stance is, "I'll not change because I'm not wrong."

Prof. Howard Hendricks notes that people have two types of needs: real needs and felt needs.5 A real need must be felt before we'll do anything about it. For instance, you could have cancer but not know it—an undetected but very real malady that needs attention. If your doctor diagnosed it, you'd become aware of the illness, feel the need, and seek treatment. Evaluation and diagnosis would transform your real need into a felt need. Unreasonable people have flaws but don't see them, so they do nothing to correct them. Frequently a client being driven crazy by an unreasonable person remarks, "He's the one who really needs to be in here getting help." That may be true, but no one seeks help without first realizing help is needed. The unreasonable person doesn't see that anything is wrong with him, so why should he seek help? Change presupposes awareness.

That's why the Mr. Potters of the world rarely come to offices like mine—they believe there's nothing wrong with them. In It's a Wonderful Life, Mr. Potter saw himself as the good guy, the smart and powerful person looking after lazy and uneducated townsfolk. Having that view of himself, why would he ever change anything?

So here's what we're up against when we have conflict with unreasonable people. They automatically assume we're the ones in the wrong, they fail to see their contributions to the conflict, they claim no responsibility for any part of the problem, they're not bothered by the impact of their words and actions on us, and they change nothing because nothing about them needs changing. Is it any wonder that unreasonable people are so difficult for us to handle?

This chart summarizes the different outcomes when the "reason muscles" are used by reasonable people and not used by unreasonable people.

Outcomes of Reason Muscle Use

Reason Muscle	When Used (Reasonable People)	When Not Used (Unreasonable People)
Humility	I could be wrong, you could be right, let's talk	I'm right, you're wrong, end of discussion
Awareness	I see where I'm wrong	I only see where I'm right
Responsibility	It bothers me when I'm wrong	If I'm wrong, so what?
Empathy	It bothers	I'm only

	me when my wrongness hurts you	bothered when your wrongness hurts me
Reliability	When I'm wrong, I'll change	I'll not change because I'm not wrong

The Unreasonable Person's Conflict Goal

When two reasonable people argue, their buttons get pushed, they react, they push buttons, they fail to use their "reason muscles," they make mistakes, and it may look and sound pretty ugly. But ultimately they are heading for the same objective: solving the problem. When a reasonable person argues with an unreasonable person, they have different objectives. The reasonable person's conflict goal is resolution while the unreasonable person's goal is rightness.

My two oldest children are girls born three years apart. They are both now extremely articulate, but when the youngest was first learning to talk, she was consistently out chattered by her loquacious older sister. Realizing her verbal disadvantage, the youngest would start swinging her fists. She hoped to accomplish physically what couldn't be accomplished verbally.

Similarly, an unreasonable person in conflict with a reasonable person is at a disadvantage because he's fighting someone who has something he doesn't possess—"reason muscles." He lacks what's necessary to do the right things with the wrongness. Therefore, he opts for a different conflict goal—rightness—which requires no wrongness acknowledgment. When the dust settles, he doesn't care about mutually satisfying problem solutions, but he does care about being right. To the unreasonable person, being right is entwined with his identity as a person and/or survival.6 He needs to eat, he needs to breathe, and he needs to be right.

The Unreasonable Person's Means of Reaching the Goal: Drama

Unable and/or unwilling to tolerate wrongness, the unreasonable person opts for the only acceptable conflict outcome to him or her—rightness—and the method used to achieve that outcome is usually drama.7 For example, suppose you're in a checkout line and the lady in front of you has two-year-old Suzie in her shopping cart. Suzie begs for something off the rack close to the register, and mom says no. Suzie asks again. Mom says no again. Suzie begs louder. Mom says no louder. Customers six aisles away have now joined you as members of the audience. The power struggle escalates to a crescendo until finally...guess what happens. Mom gives in. Suzie wins. Suzie's agitation drops considerably while Mom's agitation spikes through the stratosphere. Suzie is now the calm, good guy in control. Mom is now the exasperated bad guy who's out of control.

Lacking the maturity to reason, Suzie has just staged a drama to get what she wants and wins without using any "reason muscles." When toddlers do this, we call them spoiled brats. When adolescents do this, we call them bullies. When adults do this, we call them unreasonable people, jerks, and any of the myriad other names we come up with. In fact, dealing with an adult unreasonable person is very much like dealing with a child throwing a temper tantrum.

Some unreasonable people are openly dramatic, the kind we refer to as "drama queens" (or "drama kings") while others stage dramas in ways that are almost undetectable. Most unreasonable people missed attending Good Conflict Camp, but they all attended Drama School, where they developed into thespians of the highest order. That's why certain terms have become associated with unreasonable people: theatrics, grandstanding, mind games, soap operas.

I'm sometimes asked, "Do they know what they're doing? Do they plan out these dramas deliberately?" Good question. It's less likely that they plan them and more likely that drama has been used so routinely that it's done without conscious deliberation. Perhaps some people do both. Many unreasonable people seem to get so caught up in their drama that they lose the ability to distinguish between drama and real life.

Drama's Purpose

On March 4, 1933, Franklin Roosevelt was about to be inaugurated as president of the United States during one of the nation's most difficult periods, the Great Depression. In his thirties Roosevelt was stricken with polio, rendering his leg muscles useless. Having to rely exclusively on his arms, he developed enormous upper body strength. Leg braces, which could be locked into place, enabled him to stand upright when giving speeches.

Roosevelt knew the populace was demoralized and needed leadership that was strong, visionary, and courageous. He also understood that the picture of a president taking the oath of office from a wheelchair would not inspire confidence in a day when most people doubted the capabilities of disabled individuals. These images would be broadcast to a depressed nation using the newly developed media of the day—"talkies" or motion pictures with sound.

So Roosevelt devised a plan. After being discreetly helped from his chair, he used his powerful arms to brace himself on the arms of men on either side as they all made their way to the front. They had carefully choreographed, paced, and timed their movements in such a way that Roosevelt appeared to be walking with the group. In reality, his legs only lightly brushed the floor as he was carried along. His braces were locked into place at the podium, and he took the oath of office. To a beleaguered nation, he stood and delivered his inaugural address, which contained the confidence-inspiring line, "The only thing we have to fear is fear itself."

Here's my point. Roosevelt had atrophied muscles that were incapable of use and, had this knowledge been revealed, his leadership and survival as president would likely have been jeopardized. Therefore, he learned to act strong in places where he was actually weak. The strategy worked. And that's what the unreasonable person does. He has atrophied "reason muscles" and, if this were revealed, he'd have to admit wrongness, something he's unwilling to face because it threatens his survival. He uses drama to act strong where he is actually weak. Roosevelt performed his drama for a noble purpose—to provide strong national leadership. The unreasonable person performs his drama for self-serving reasons—to maintain rightness and avoid wrongness.

Chapter 8: The Martyr Employee Or 'Victim'

Who they are: This is your 'woe is me' employee. Everyone has the same amount of work to do but to listen to this employee you would think that he or she was doing everyone else's work as well as her own. A martyr likes nothing better than complaining, whining, bitching and moaning to anyone who will listen about how much work, pressure and responsibility they have on their shoulders. Often, they believe they cannot get a task done because of something that is out of their control. In short, they have no 'get-up-and-go' or positive attitude.

A victim often comes across as tentative, apprehensive and helpless. They too are likely to blame others for their lack of productivity and efficiency. What's more, they bring everyone else down. In short, they are depressing.

You'll also notice that when they attempt to explain themselves, they will invariably leave out the key one or two details that would explain why they haven't been able to finish their work. Instead of honestly wanting to get to the bottom of a problem, they will invoke the 'woe is me' defence. 'Why does it always happen to me?'

What to do: The best way to deal with a martyr or victim is to listen and empathise – these people are often ignored and feel neglected – and try to get him or her to prioritise their problems. Once they have narrowed down the real problem, discuss with them an appropriate plan to solve it. Encourage the employee to focus on the future and not the past, and try to help them find ways to win some short-term successes to boost their confidence and convince themselves they are not helpless.

If all else fails, however, be ready to take a harder line: tell them that you will not listen to their complaints if they have no plan for a solution, warn them off for timewasting and be honest: tell them that they are damaging the morale of their team mates. Let them know that excuses and moans will not be tolerated; only results matter.

The Absentee Worker

Who they are: We all have sick days now and then; we even all have days when we just can't face going into work. Yes, even us bosses too. However, there's a very big difference between thinking about throwing a sickie and actually doing it. The absentee worker will take more sick days than would seem reasonably normal; they may seem to lurch from one supposed health or personal crisis to another. As I said in our motivation chapter, absenteeism costs UK industry £11.5bn annually.

So, if you have a repeat absentee offender, how can you handle it?

What to do: The first thing you need to do is to assess the reason behind the absence. Is the employee genuinely ill, for instance? A doctor's note should tell you that. If the employee takes a lot of odd days off here and there – for which they can self-certificate and don't need a doctor's note – that should raise a red flag.

Legally in the UK, you can't ask for medical evidence or a fit note (Statement of Fitness to Work) – the new sick note – until someone has been away from work for more than seven days. However, the seven days do include weekends and bank holidays and any other days the employee usually does not work. If your company does not have a formal sickness procedure as yet, it is good practice to ask for the fit note after this time as standard.

For all other sick days of seven days or less, make a point of asking people to self-certificate. This is when they have to fill in and sign an official form giving information about their illness, along with the dates the sickness started and ended. This has the bonus of bringing home to the worker that their sick days are being monitored.

Likewise, make sure that each employee knows what action is expected of them if they are ill or want to claim a sick day. It is advisable to tell them that they must telephone in person to speak to their line manager direct (no, their mother/ wife/ husband/ flatmate or next door neighbour cannot do it for them unless they are very ill and in hospital); they should not leave a message, nor should they email.

They should also call as soon as they are able and telephone each and every morning that they are sick. They should not call once and then be off for three days. If nothing else, the demand that people call in each morning not only allows the manager to know how to use their cover effectively, but it also helps to dissuade those who are not genuine from going through with throwing a sickie in the first place. You can even carry out a return to work interview after sickness to further discourage people from taking advantage.

Here's a tricky situation: what do you do if an employee asked for and was refused a certain day off, but coincidentally takes it 'off sick' anyway? You strongly suspect that there was nothing actually wrong with them but, of course, you can't prove it. It's a tough one. Lying about being sick is a definite disciplinary matter, but that only works if you can prove the employee lied (for example, if they were seen out at a bar instead). If you strongly suspect that he or she lied, however, and particularly if they have a history of it, you should investigate further.

Question the employee when he or she originally calls in sick and conduct a return to work interview when they return. Ask the employee for an explanation. If they have done this before, point out the pattern and again ask for their explanation. In many cases, this interview may be enough to prevent any future occurrence once they know you are watching them. If you have a reasonable belief that the absence was not genuine as a result of their response, you are entitled to start disciplinary action, whether you want to start by giving a verbal or written warning.

In order to avoid an unfair dismissal claim, however, you must be sure to carry out a proper investigation first and not just jump to conclusions. Remember the burden of proof at all times; you want to have enough information to convince a court that you were disciplining in good faith should you need to. If there is an underlying health issue or potential disability discrimination issues, this is doubly important.

Once your company has an attendance policy in place that every employee is aware of, you can confront regular offenders using an objective system of monitoring and measuring.

Of course, while having an absenteeism policy is important, it may not be tackling the crux of the problem. By far the biggest reason for absenteeism without a legitimate medical complaint is demotivation and stress; re-read the motivation section again for advice on how to inspire and motivate your staff. Even your management style could be an influence when it comes to absenteeism; autocratic and authoritarian managers tend to encourage higher levels of sickness than their more democratic counterparts.

Otherwise, treat all sickness in a sympathetic manner. Don't automatically assume employees are swinging the lead; a great many sick days will be legitimate.

But here's a dilemma for you: what do you do if the person is genuinely ill but has such a lot of sick time that you and your department are struggling to cope? It's a moral as well as a business decision, but should you – and could you – let them go?

Legally there is no requirement for the company to rehabilitate a sick worker; however, you need to know your law on this one because you may have legal responsibilities and limitations under the Disability Discrimination Act, the Health and Safety at Work Act 1974, the Employment Rights Act 1966 and the Employment Act 2002 (Dispute Regulations) 2004. It's probably best to consult HR, I think.

In the meantime, let's look at a typical conversation with a repeat absentee offender who you suspect isn't really ill as often as they claim. In this scenario, the employee has rung the manager to let them know they will be off ill for a few days. How should the manager respond?

Chapter 9: The Guilt Tripper

Guilt tripping is actually one of the most manipulative techniques that people use to get what they want. When a person is able to make you feel guilty, it is possible to get almost anything from you. However, do not consider using guilt tripping on other people because this technique can actually wear out other people and you may end up losing their respect.

Recognize the telltale signs

One of the most effect techniques in dealing with people who like to use guilt trip is to stop it at an early stage. Do not allow yourself to be sucked in by other people's guilt trips. You can do this by learning how to spot people who use guilt trip on you. When another person starts talking to you with the words "If you were more reliable, you would..." or "If you truly care for me, you would...", be wary because the other person may be pushing you in in one of his guilt trips. Underneath these sentences, the other person is really trying to tell you to do what they want you to do. Guilt trippers also love to induce a guilt trip by telling you exactly what you would not do. For instance, "I knew what I heard is wrong. I know you will never start a new project without discussing it with me first." In that statement, the other person has actually told you what he wants you to do which is to discuss all projects with him before you start anything.

Turn the guilt back to the other person

When someone makes you feel guilty just to get what he wants, you can use the same approach on him so that he will understand the consequence of his actions. When another person attempts to manipulate you using guilt, you can respond by telling him how he is not caring for, appreciating or respecting your behavior towards him. When you do this, you will be able to end the need to satisfy the obligation that the other person is imposing on you. For instance, when a colleague tells you that you do not seem to care about the efforts that he has been doing to help you, you can tell him that you really care and it seems that it is he who doesn't appreciate how much you care. When he replies that he appreciates your care, you can reply back that it is the same with you and that you appreciate his efforts.

Reduce a guilt tripper's hold on you

When a guilt tripper attempts to manipulate you by making a suggestion that he does not seem to matter to you, do not buy into his manipulation. You can opt to simply reply with a quick retort that ends the manipulation immediately. One example of a guilt trip statement is:"It is alright. You can just choose X to be part of the new project while I clean up his mess in this unfinished project. Do not worry about me, I am fine."You can cut the manipulation by simply saying,"That's wonderful! I am so happy that you are fine with finishing the old project. I really appreciate it, thanks!"

Move the assumption statement away from you

Assumption statements normally start with"I guess"or"I wish"or"I suppose". A couple of examples are "I wish the management understands how difficult it is for me to continue working in this task"or"I suppose I can be included in the list of people up for promotion since I have made the biggest contribution to the team this year." Guilt trippers love using assumption statements because they are not actually asking a question which they do not like to do since it causes them to feel like they are losing control. When you are dealing with a more decent person, he will ask questions in order to know what you are really doing and then he will proceed with a conversation based on the information that you give. A guilt tripper, on the other hand, will simply give his assumptions on what you are doing in order to allow him to manipulate you. He wants you to do what he assumes you will do instead of waiting to listen to what you really want to do. Here is how you can deflect assumption statements away from you:

Guilt Tripper:"I wish I can be included in the list of people up for promotion since I have made the biggest contribution to the team this year."

You:"The management team will make that decision based on company policies."

Guilt Tripper:"I suppose you will not support me and you will not recommend my promotion."

You:"You know that I recommend all my subordinates who have excellent performance. Your credentials will be reviewed by the management team to see if you will qualify for the promotion."

Guilt Tripper:"If you do not think that my performance will not qualify me for promotion, you do not really need to waste your time giving me a recommendation."

You:"I am glad that you understand the policies of the company with regardto promotions."

Do not join a guilt tripper when he is playing mind games using other people

Some guilt trippers will not want you to think that they are imposing their will on you; hence, they will use other people as reference of authority. When they want you to do something, they will tell you that they know an uncle or another successful person who has done that particular thing before with positive results. A guilt tripper will use this strategy when he senses that you are not responsive to the manipulations that he is doing.

Continuing with our previous example, the guilt tripper could carry on with his agenda by saying that the manager of the other department thinks that he is ripe for promotion and his outputs are much better than those of most otherpeople in the organization. By saying this, the guilt tripper relinquishes his own responsibility for uttering the statements that he really wants you to hear. You can cut the manipulation by saying:"I did not realize that the manager of the other department is fully aware of all aspects of your performance. I think I need to talk to her to discuss this with her."

Avoid being confronted by a guilt tripper

You need to be very wary when dealing with guilt trippers. These people normally use schemes or mind games to create disputes or conflicts with you when they do not get what they want. When a guilt tripper senses that you are not falling to his subtle hints, he will use disputes and conflicts to gain control over you. A guilt tripper can utilize confrontational statements with the objective of upsetting you so that you will enter into an argument with him. He can tell you, "You have never really been supportive of me. You always disregard my efforts. I am invisible to you." Instead of entering into an argument with the guilt tripper, you can simply reply with a "no" and then point out objective facts. Respond calmly and rationally to the guilt tripper. Do not provoke an argument by frowning or answering back. Try your best to keep your responses friendly and simple.

Dodge the self-pity

When you hear a guilt tripper tell you that everything is so unfair for him and that he seems to be doing nothing right, he is actually trying to get your sympathy so that he can use it in the future for his own advantage. When you fall into his trap, the guilt tripper will depend on his weakness to seek all kinds of help from you including emotional assistance and financial help. Watch out for statements and attitudes that tell you "Oh, you are the only one I can really depend on" or "You are the only one who truly listens to me". When a colleague starts his self-pity scheme on you, be sympathetic but still be cautious because you do not really want to be fully obligated to him. You can reply with "You know that is not true. You can talk to the HR manager and directly to our department head if you have any issues and concerns," or "I know that x and y will also be willing to listen to you and help with what they can."

Be wary of people who change and alter facts in order to make them look more attractive

In general, these people will resort to lying to obtain what they want from other people. You can always see this in the workplace because people would want to get their colleagues on their side or to look good in front of higher authorities. When you know that you have been given a distorted fact, always ask for clarifications. Be frank in saying that that is not how you recall the facts and you hope to better understand the situation, but always remain respectful and polite. Simply say that you want the clarification because you are confused. Pose basic questions about the agreement that you have come up with and how the other person believes the agreement was reached. Use the guilt tripper's answers in straightening the facts. You should also be cautious of people who seem to have "selective memories" because this is another tool to manipulate and control others. Some people use selective memory to wriggle out of responsibilities that they don't want to take while still being able to remember the responsibilities that they want to do.

Do not become a victim of guilt trippers who use "love" as a tool to bargain

Some guilt trippers will use the following statements to manipulate you into giving them what they want: "Because you know I love you, do this and this and this for me..." or "I know that you really love me, so do this and this and this..." This type of manipulation is commonly used in relationships and friendships but it can be altered a bit in order to work in the office environment. Guilt trippers who show this kind of attitude normally want you to feel obligated. Don't worry; you can prevent people close to you from manipulating your love and care for them by pointing out how your existing actions already prove how much you love them. You can get better results by being more compassionate and telling them how much you appreciate their love and care for you as well. When a subordinate tells you to do something to prove that you care for his welfare, you can reply that you do care for his welfare and that is why you are doing the things that you are currently doing. Do not be shy in enumerating the good things that you actually do for your subordinates.

Uncover the fake illnesses that guilt trippers love to fabricate

It is quite unfortunate that some guilt trippers will go to the extent of using illness as a means to manipulate other people. Some guilt trippers stick to minor sickness and symptoms to get other people's sympathy, but theyactually suffer from Munchausen's Syndrome or Factitious Disorder. These guilt trippers will fake their sickness by intentionally producing fake and exaggerated symptoms in order to obtain what they want. Some guilt trippers do this just to avoid fulfilling their obligations and to have more time for leisure and recreation while others do this to take advantage of their medical benefits. Still some people are really just very lazy that they always want other people to do their tasks for them.

If you notice that a colleague or a subordinate is always using this scheme, you can start considering whether he really requires medical help from a psychologist or a psychiatrist because he may already be suffering from Factitious Disorder. If the other person is indeed suffering from Factitious Disorder, you should avoid being judgmental. People normally acquire the disorder as their way of responding to stress until it has turned into a disruptive behavior. To show your compassion, you can give a suggestion that the other person consult a mental health expert who can help him with his worries and anxieties, but avoid being aggressive about the other person's fake illnesses.

Ignore guilt trippers who manipulate your emotions through their emotional outbursts

There are guilt trippers will use screaming, sorrow, crying and other forms of emotions to get what they want from other people. We can normally see this in young kids and adolescents who use emotional outbursts to manipulate their parents and other adults to give them what they want. When you notice that a colleague or a subordinate constantly uses his emotional outbursts to get you to do what he wants, you need to be firm in saying no. But always remain calm and polite. You can show compassion by suggesting that the other person seek help from a mental health expert who can help him better deal with his emotions.

Listen to your own self

When you are dealing with a guilt tripper, you should learn how to listen to your own self so you can determine your own thoughts and feelings about the situation. You need to assess whether the behaviors of the other person is making you feel pressured, oppressed and obligated to give in to what the other person wants but you do not really want to do. Allow your own thoughts and emotions to guide you to where you want your relationship with the guilt tripper to go to.

Chapter 10: The Practical Ways To Win Difficult People Over Or To Apply In Dealing With Them.

UNDERSTAND THE PERSON

Like it has been said in chapter two that understanding has a lot do with life situations. To deal with a difficult person, you must try to understand the person and certain things concerning him or her. There is always a cause to every problem. And if you must deal with any problem and successfully overcome it, you must first of all locate the cause.

You do it like this; What are the things that easily gets the person annoyed or pissed off? What are the person's likes or dislikes? Taking cognizance of these two important points will help you to understand the person better.

You can remember how I dealt with my difficult room-mate. After you have understood the person's likes and dislikes, the next thing to do is to look for ways to avoid the dislikes and try to do only those things that are his/her likes.

STUDY THE PERSON'S GOOD SIDES AND DEVELOP A KIND OF LIKENESS AND INTEREST IN THEM.

A difficult person isn't a bad person. Being difficult is not being wicked. No matter how difficult a person is, he or she will have the good sides. A person can be difficult and at the same time, be passionate. My room-mate, though, doesn't joke with money, still he tries to help when he sees someone in need. This is one of the good sides of him that I developed interest in.

So, to deal with someone difficult, you must observe the positive sides of him/her, then channel your likeness to it. This will help you more in getting along with the person.

IGNORE THE BAD SIDES

Overlooking the bad acts of a difficult person can be helpful at times. This doesn't mean you should become a fool or you shouldn't call the person to iron out issues. It literarily means you shouldn't take offence all the time. You should always try to overlook minor offences. If there is a part of him/her that you must ignore just to make peace reign, then do so if you are not really affected.

The last time before I wrote this book, I asked a girl if ignoring the bad sides of a difficult person can help solve the problem, she said HELL NO. She said she can't bare being wronged or being looked down on. And that she will always look into the eyes of anyone who feels she can be ridden on. Then I asked that; what if it were a boss at work and the pay is very high and scarce to get. And she was like she will look for ways to handle him. Then I said this is what I'm saying. When it is a must for you to concur, ignore the bad side to have your way.

CHEER UP THE GOOD SIDES

One easy way to get along with someone who seem to be difficult is to applaud his/her achievements or give kudos when necessary. You can even appreciate those little good things you observe that he/she does to you or to others. Doing this will allow the person to develop more interest in you and see you as someone he/she can rely on or talk to when the need arises.

Cheering up the good sides is not that you should be hypocritical. It doesn't mean you applaud a bad act or try to defend a wrong cause or wrong deeds of the person or try to motivate him to do more.

Cheering up the good sides simply means spotting the positive sides and telling the person to do more and how he/she can do more. You can win a very difficult person by doing this.

FLOW WITH THE ATMOSPHERE

An important issue discussed with an important person under a right and cool atmosphere brings at resounding results.

What do I mean by flowing with the atmosphere? Try to discuss an issue with an unhappy or angry man and I assure that you must expect failure. If you really need to discuss an important issue, make complaints, or give suggestion to someone who is difficult or anybody at all, you must observe the person's mood and make sure the current mood is conducive and palatable for such discussion.

Take for instance; trying to eat a food that has just left the cooker in 30secs will actually burn the tongue. If you must eat the food, then you will have to wait till it gets cooler and become eatable.

Same applies to dealing with anybody too. A bad mood cannot solve problems. If you want your suggestions or request to be attended to, you must tender it at the right time under a right atmosphere.

BE MATURE OR ACT MATURELY

Your words, acts, behaviors, characters, dealings and gesture must be mature. Maturity is more of exhibiting understanding and choosing the right words to use.

The maturity you display in dealing with anybody can force him/her to respect you regardless of your age. I have been doing this and it has working for me.

When you don't reply harsh words with harsh words, when you strictly follow orders as an employee, when you do the right you ought to do at the right time, everyone around will give you respect without you demanding it form them. Even a difficult person will too.

BE SINCERE AND TRUSTWORTHY

Let your yes be yes and your no be no. In any relationship at any level, being trusted and sincerity have a long way to go in every life. To be loved, respected, regarded, honored and accepted in any form of relationship or gathering, these tow must be in place.

If everyone is complaining of a certain difficult person wherever you find yourself, make sure you prove your sincerity and trustworthiness, and you will find out that all of those complaining have gotten it wrong. For the person will single you out and develop likeness in you.

Especially in love relationships, these two are very important. They are the ones that will speak for you when distance comes in. They will also make a lover that seems difficult become soft. That is if there is true love. Because if there isn't true love, no matter how high your level of sincerity is, you will only be wasting your time and effort. If a difficult lover refuses to change with time, after all your efforts, then back out!!!.

AVOID BEING TO CLOSE OR TOO FAR

Balancing the scale with some certain difficult people can help at times. Another way to deal with difficult people is to avoid choking them with too much of closeness or going too far from them. This you must do if it is a must for you, like a place of work or an organization you belong to.

When you sense that your closeness to someone is always causing problems then decrease it. And when the person starts complaining of you running away, then get a little bit close. Greetings and few minutes of checking on can solve the whole problem.

Dealing with certain difficult people at time requires wisdom. You have to give it all it takes to avoid problems and misunderstandings.

FRY YOUR EGO

Humility pays a lot. Being proud, uncontrollable, feeling big, and being not submissive has no gain. Those that are humble and submissive are most likely to get more followers and make more friends.

Frying your ego in dealing with dealing with different personalities will make them respect you.

When you greet someone who has wronged you first, when you greet some who has vowed not to greet you, when you tell the person who has offended you — "sorry", when you greet someone younger or junior to you firstly, you are ignorantly earning the badge of more respect.

Difficult people are not blind. For they can see everything going around too. They can tell of other people's personalities too. So, when you have been carefully observed by them that you are humble, they will actually develop interest in you and you become good friends.

Frying your ego is maturity reflective. Doing this, you are reflecting maturity and understanding of life.

USE THE RIGHT WORDS

This method has been explained chapter four. You can flip back to master the power of words as briefly discussed there. It is a great tool in handling difficult people.

BUY THE PERSON GIFTS, BOOKS, OR EDUCATIONAL MATERIALS

Your gift will pave way for you in life. This is not a new a new method to win hearts or win someone over.

When people see how much you love and care for them, they cherish it and reciprocate specially for you and you alone. Though they may still seem to be difficult in the sight of others but not towards you.

Have you ever heard a husband defending his wife when people are complaining of her being difficult to move with? Have you also heard friends defending their friends whom people are complaining of? It is not that those complaining are wrong but because those defending them have a way of winning them over.

Imagine not forgetting a difficult person's birthday or important dates and trying your best to present a gift to them.

You can imagine buying them educational or motivational books to cheer them up in their career or hustle. Or getting them materials that will help them not to give up in dream chasing. This is a good method of winning any heart over.

WARNING: If a lover seems not to be appreciative no matter what you do to please him/her, then the problem is not being difficult but not being in love with you. That is if you have no previous record of cheating of offence that you haven't ironed out.

INVITE THE FOR IMPORTANT SEMINARS OR SPIRITUAL TEACHINGS

Like I said that words are powerful and can change anyone. A difficult person can easily change by listening to powerful messages and seminars from any gathering.

People often change mostly when someone they cherish a lot due to impacts or achievements is saying things concerning them or concerning life generally.

Authoritative words from wise speakers can change any unrepentant soul or hardened heart. You can get along with difficult people by inviting them to places or seminars where they can learn one or two things concerning life or business. And apart from getting along, they can easily change.

THEN, YOU CAN PRAY FOR THEM

Previously, you have learnt about the power of prayer, that prayers can change any situation, solve any problem and also change any heart.

Going down on your knees to pray for another person usually attracts God's attention. God is love and when he sees someone who is showing love to another fellow being like him in the place of prayer, he honors such unselfish prayers.

He even commands us to love our neighbor as ourselves. God honors the prayers offered for someone else or on behalf someone else for it shows love.

The prayer you pray on your knees without the person's consent can do the wonders you expect. No difficult heart has power over prayer.

These are the 13 super practical ways to deal with any difficult person.

We have come to the conclusion of this chapter and by extension, to the conclusion of this book. I sincerely believe you've learnt so many things as regards dealing with difficult people and how to handle situations that have to do with them.

You can put the steps and method discussed and exposed in this book to practice and you will marvel at the positive result you will be getting.

Wishing you a happy and smooth relationship with everyone. Thanks for your precious time. Don't forget- "Always try to locate the cause of a problem and start dealing with it from there".

Chapter 11: How To Deal With A Difficult Customer And Provide Great Customer Service

Whether you work in an office building, or in retail, at one point or another, you will have to deal with a difficult customer. They are agitated and upset and you happened to be the lucky employee who stepped up to help them. In order to deal with a difficult customer, you must first remain calm and avoid taking the anger of the customer personally. It's difficult to solve problems under stress. It's important for the customer service representative to recognize that the anger being expressed is the result of the situation and the customer's frustration. The next step is to acknowledge the customer's anger and frustration. This is a crucial step. In many cases being listened to and acknowledged is the main thing that angry customers are seeking. Customer service representatives can let the customer know that they are being heard as well as ensure that they understand the nature of the problem correctly. You can do this by repeating the main part of the problem back to the customer and confirming its accuracy. It's important to apologize to the customer without offering excuses or trying to shift blame, even if there are good excuses and blame belongs elsewhere. These initial responses will defuse the anger of many customers.

Next, it's important to identify whether the customer wants the problem solved, wants compensation or wants both. Ideally, one could provide both, but in some cases, such as a gift failing to arrive on time or a bowl of soup spilled on the lap of a diner, it is no longer possible to rectify the initial issue. When at all feasible, however, the customer service representative should focus on solving the problem as described by the customer. Compensation can be tricky. Customers who are skilled negotiators may already have a form of compensation in mind. This can actually make one's job easier if the compensation is a reasonable one such as a comped restaurant meal for unsatisfactory food or service. However, the customer may demand unreasonable compensation. In this case one must be diplomatic in negotiating with the customer to agree to a reasonable amount of compensation that the customer still feels is adequate. It's still a good idea, though, to ask the customer what action would make them happy. The customer should begin to feel as though you are no longer an adversary but an ally in working to solve the problem. The customer service representative might use inclusive language like "we" to discuss the issue such as "What can we do to resolve this?" A customer who demands impossible solutions or compensation should be reassured that you are doing everything in one's power to solve the issue. Also state that you will continue working with the customer until the issue is resolved to everyone's satisfaction. Throughout the interaction, it's important to continue treating the customer like a fellow human being. Empathy is vital. Often, the anger of a customer comes from feeling powerless. Depending on the nature of the problem and what is at stake, it may also arise from understandable fears and frustrations. Putting oneself in the customer's shoes and working to fix the situation from that viewpoint can provide valuable insight and the very best customer service.

With these strategies, you can hope to diffuse the anger of a difficult customer and help solve their problems. As you work together with the customer, you can change a negative experience with your company into a positive one.

Conclusion

Thank you again for downloading this book!

I hope this book was able to help you to develop skills and strategies needed to deal with difficult people at work.

The next step would be to apply these steps and these tips as necessary in your current work situation. Don't let bullies, gossip mongers, and perpetual pessimists stop you from achieving your ultimate work goals.

www.ingramcontent.com/pod-product-compliance
Lightning Source LLC
Chambersburg PA
CBHW071456070526
44578CB00001B/359